Renaissance Dogs

Taylor Wagmore, a professor of cynology (the scientific study of dogs) at Great Dane University in Texas, is very much a 'dog person' – and proud. He lives in Houston, often called the 'dog capital of America' due to its high dog-to-human ratio and dog-friendly reputation. He shares his home with two chocolate Labradors, Barry and Carl. Oh, and a wife and two children.

For Barry and Carl.

First published in Great Britain in 2025
by Greenfinch
An imprint of Quercus
Part of John Murray Group

Copyright © 2025 Malcolm Croft

The moral right of Malcolm Croft to be identified as the author of this work has been asserted in accordance with the Copyright, Designs and Patents Act, 1988.

All rights reserved. No part of this publication may be reproduced or transmitted in any form or by any means, electronic or mechanical, including photocopy, recording, or any information storage and retrieval system, without permission in writing from the publisher.

A CIP catalogue record for this book is available from the British Library

HB ISBN 978-1-52944-966-2
Ebook ISBN 978-1-52944-967-9

10 9 8 7 6 5 4 3 2 1

Cover and interior design by James Pople

Artworks supplied by Alamy: 2, 7, 21, 26, 28, 36, 53, 57, 63, 66,72, 74, 75, 76, 94, 108, 121, 136, 138,140, 142, 145, 146, 151, 154, 161,163, 190, 200, 204.

Printed and bound in Estonia by OU Print Best

Papers used by Quercus are from well-managed forests and other responsible sources.

Quercus
Carmelite House
50 Victoria Embankment
London EC4Y 0DZ

John Murray Group
Part of Hodder & Stoughton Limited
An Hachette UK company

The authorised representative in the EEA is Hachette Ireland, 8 Castlecourt Centre, Dublin 15, D15 XTP3, Ireland (email: info@hbgi.ie)

Renaissance Dogs

Curious canines from a bygone age

Professor Taylor Wagmore

greenfinch

CONTENTS

Introduction 6

1. Release the Hounds! 9

2. Old Dogs, Old Tricks 29

3. Sleeping Dogs Lie 49

4. The Doghouse 69

5. Beware of the Dog 89

6. Hot Doggin' 109

7. Every Dog Has its Day (Off) 129

8. Barking Up the Wrong Tree 149

9. Hounds of Love 169

10. Hair of the Dog 189

Portrait of Duchess Katharina von Mecklenburg (and half-shaved) dog, *1514, by Lucas Cranach the Elder. © Staatliche Kunstsammlungen Dresden/Bridgeman Images.*

INTRODUCTION

Ah, the Renaissance. The Golden Age. If you're looking for humanity's greatest hits – art, astronomy, literature, science, education, medicine, etc. – the moments when we truly pulled our fingers out from the smelly crevices of the Middle Ages, then the Renaissance is it. Between 1400 and 1700(ish) – we've thrown in a little Reformation and Enlightenment-era art too because, well, why not – opening your eyes in the morning was transformed from a rather bleak experience to being a quite pleasant one, all thanks to a wealth of life-changing inventions: the pencil, the microscope, the telescope, the printing press and even the flushable toilet. These instruments truly dragged us from the Dark Ages into the light. And, boy, what a breath of fresh air it was.

The Renaissance was so revolutionary, in fact, that it birthed the discovery of gravity. (Before Isaac Newton came along in 1666, everything was just floating in the air for no reason at all, which is crazy when you think about it.) Newton was just one of many magnificent mortals who defined these immortal times. Shakespeare, da Vinci, Galilei, Machiavelli, Copernicus, Magellan, Bacon, Petrarch... and that guy who mistook America for India... all ran so the rest of us could now walk. Sure, the Renaissance

INTRODUCTION

had its downsides – the constant warring, the never-ending pestilence, and eternal religious persecution – but let's forget about that. Ooh, look – a cute little doggy!

By our side every step of the way through this crazy period were, of course, dogs. Forever loyal and loving, these faithful companions and protectors witnessed humankind's first steps towards greatness, without ever once complaining about our smell when we were too busy to take a shower (invented

in 1767, FYI), despite having the most powerful noses on the planet. That's love, right there. For three centuries or so, these furry, four-legged friends, with their dedication to pure joy and play (and eating literally anything that isn't nailed down), have taught us how to be a little less like a wild animal and a little more like them. This dog-eared collection of canines – a *dogalogue*, if you'll permit – celebrates these colourful creatures in all their silliest shapes and sizes.

As repayment for their service and loyalty during this period, the world's greatest art masters painted pooches, poodles and pups ever more imaginatively, and often ridiculously, into every frame of our lives – through the painting techniques the era pioneered (Google it, I'm running out of space here). This ensured their place in the pantheon of recorded history alongside us, even if they didn't sit still for one second of it.

So, welcome to the Renaissance. Grab a shovel, because you're about to scoop up a *lot* of silly doggy fun. Now, tell me, which Renaissance dog is *your* favourite?

1.
RELEASE THE HOUNDS!

DURING THE RENAISSANCE, doggies of all shapes and sizes grew significantly in number and types of breeds, thanks to humanity's newfound passion for international 'travel' (read: colonisation). Let's go for a walk through history and let these dogs off their leash…

A dog patiently waiting for walkies, St. Augustine in His Study, 1502, by Vittore Carpaccio. © Andrea Jemolo/Bridgeman Images.

RENAISSANCE DOGS

'I'll pray too, Mum. "Dear Lord, I want sausages for dinner. Amen."'

Praying woman with her dog, *c.1480, by Hans Memling.*
© *Fine Art Images/Bridgeman Images.*

Meaning 'rebirth' in French, the Renaissance was a period in European civilisation that followed the rather medieval Middle Ages. It was characterised by a profound rediscovery of ancient classical learning and wisdom, leading to the development of new laws and principles in fields such as architecture, education, medicine and art.

RELEASE THE HOUNDS!

'A monkey, Mum! I wanna chase it! Can I chase it? Can I? Can I? Can I?'

Portrait of a lady with a dog (and a monkey), *1700*, by
Nicolas de Largillière. Wikimedia Commons.

RENAISSANCE DOGS

'I poop in *one* bed and now everyone's making a big deal about it.'

St. Augustine Reading Rhetoric and
Philosophy at the School of Rome, *1464, by
Benozzo Gozzoli. Bridgeman Images.*

RELEASE THE HOUNDS!

'So, this is my family. My two dads are a bit weird, but I love them.'

Altarpiece of the Parliament of Paris, c.1500, by the French School. © Photo Josse/Bridgeman Images.

'You look busy. I'll take myself for a walk.'

The Flagellation of Christ, 1478, by Paul Lautensack.
Bridgeman Images.

'A good dog deserves a good bone.'

Ben Jonson, *A Tale of a Tub*, 1633.

RELEASE THE HOUNDS!

'There's a baby angel fondling a boob. And I'm the weird one?'

Venus with Organist (and a wonky-eyed dog), *1550, by Tiziano Vecellio. Wikimedia Commons.*

'Get out of here, damn cat! This is my page.'

RELEASE THE HOUNDS!

'Just because I look guilty doesn't mean I am...honest.'

Adoration of the Magi, 1520, by Defendente Ferrari. The J. Paul Getty Museum.

'You're looking at her looking at me, looking at you, looking at her, looking at me, looking at you.'

Vanity, *central panel from the* Triptych of Earthly Vanity and Divine Salvation, *c.1485 by Hans Memling, Bridgeman Images.*

RENAISSANCE DOGS

'The runt of the litter? First one on the left, obviously.'

Portrait of Bianca degli Utili Maselli with her children, *c.1604, by Lavinia Fontana*.

―

'I would rather see the portrait of a dog that I know, than all the allegorical paintings they can show me in the world.'

Samuel Johnson, 1763.

2.
OLD DOGS, OLD TRICKS

HE RENAISSANCE REPRESENTED humanity's rediscovery of a desire to learn new and exciting things and generally to make their world a better place. For dogs, however, it was very much a case of business as usual: sleeping, playing, eating, pooping, sniffing butts and, well, you get the picture…

He's behind me, isn't he?, The Two Women, 1455, *by Vittore Carpaccio.*

'All together now, "How much is that doggy in the window?"'

Portrait of an Extraordinary Musical Dog, 1748, by Philip Reinagle. Virginia Museum of Fine Arts.

In 1413, Edward of Norwich, the 2nd Duke of York, published *The Master of Game*. It's considered the oldest English-language book on hunting and detailed the virtues and traits of hunting hounds. 'Every man shuld have a dogge to help him to hunt and to do other diverse uses,' he wrote. The book also contains the first written record of the proverb, 'It is hard to make an old dog stoop', an earlier form of 'You can't teach an old dog new tricks.'

OLD DOGS, OLD TRICKS

'If I pooped right now, would the painter have to paint my poop?'

Portrait of a lady and a young boy, 1635, by English School.
© Christie's Images/Bridgeman Images.

RENAISSANCE DOGS

'Dad, stop it! You're embarrassing me!'

Peasants Celebrating Twelfth Night, *1635, by David Teniers the Younger. National Gallery of Art, London.*

'I'm just popping out for a walk, anybody need anything?'

The Martyrdom of St Sebastian, *c. 1430, by artist unknown.*

'I'm a bad dog that deserves a good spanking.'

'I'm not shy! I just don't want to be in your stupid painting!'

Portrait of Anna Eleanora Sanvitale (aged four), *1563, by Giuseppe Mazzola Bedoli. Mondadori Portfolio/Electa/Antonio Guerra/Bridgeman Images.*

OLD DOGS, OLD TRICKS

'OK, you've had your fun, now give me the damn biscuit.'

Portrait of a Family, 1663, by Jacob Ochtervelt. © Harvard Art Museums/ Gift of F.F. Sherman in memory of his brother/Bridgeman Images.

'Give a dog an ill name and his work is done.'

John Stevens, 1706.

RENAISSANCE DOGS

'I'm a freak of nature? That's rich coming from a giraffe!'

Kangaroo-shaped dog, Garden of Earthly Delights, 1495, by Hieronymus Bosch. Wikimedia Commons.

'All dogs go to Heaven, right?'

Archangel Raphael with Tobias, *1475–80, by Biagio d'Antonio. Samuel H. Kress Collection.*

OLD DOGS, OLD TRICKS

Legend has it that in the late 1600s, Sir Isaac Newton's favourite dog, Diamond, caused a fire by knocking over a candle, destroying manuscripts containing notes from two decades of his scientific experiments. Newton is famously quoted as exclaiming, 'O Diamond, thou little knowest the mischief thou hast done!'

RENAISSANCE DOGS

OLD DOGS, OLD TRICKS

'It really pisses me off that I'm in none of these paintings.'

Man of Science Making Measurements on a Globe, 1612, by Frans Francken the Younger. © Johnny Van Haeften Ltd, London/Bridgeman Images.

3.
SLEEPING DOGS LIE

RENOWNED FOR THEIR love of a long, dreamy nap, Renaissance dogs liked nothing more than curling up in a nice warm spot at the end of the bed, utterly exhausted from all the mischief and mayhem they'd caused that day.

A lazy dog who couldn't be bothered to pose, Prince Philip Prospero, 1659, by Diego Rodriguez de Silva y Velazquez. Bridgeman Images.

'Yes, OK, it was me. I humped your pillow.'

Cain and Abel, *1474, by Bernardo di Stefano Rosselli. Wikimedia Commons.*

RENAISSANCE DOGS

'All the ladies love me.'

The Visitation, 1480, by Juan de Segovia,
Master of Miraflores/Spanish School.

'Can we do
this another day?
I'm dog-tired.'

SLEEPING DOGS LIE

'I'll sniff your butt *clean.*'

Portrait of Ivan Draškovic, *Trakošća Castle, northern Croatia, 1584, by artist unknown. Imgur.*

'I'm sorry for ripping your trousers, Dad, but they smelled weirdly delicious.'

Saint Roch, *the patron saint of dogs, 1596, by Andrea Lilio.*

———

In his 1674 book, *The Gentleman's Recreation in Four Parts*, Nicholas Cox catalogued dozens of the era's most popular dog names. Among our favourites are: Banger, Captain, Drunkard, Fuddle, Jocky, Mopsie, Ringwood, Rover, Spanker, Tunewel and Vulcan.

RENAISSANCE DOGS

'I'm her guard dog. Take one step closer and I'll nibble your ankles.'

A Child in Ecclesiastical Dress, 1660, by Juan Bautista Martínez del Mazo. Purchased with funds from the Libbey Endowment, Gift of Edward Drummond Libbey, Toledo Museum of Arts.

'There's no place else I'd rather be.'

A portrait of a girl with dog, *1562, by Francesco Torbido. © Collection of the Duke of Northumberland/Bridgeman Images.*

'Ergh! Have you just farted?'

'Paint me with a hangdog expression— it'll make me look cool.'

Portrait of a Lady with a Lapdog, *1505, by Lorenzo Costa.*

In 1533, Anne Boleyn, King Henry VIII's second wife, had a dog named Purkoy. It's believed the dog was named after the French word '*pourquoi*' (meaning 'why') due to its inquisitive nature. True to form, the curious dog died after falling from a window.

RENAISSANCE DOGS

'Best seat in the house.'

Count Giacomo Durazzo and Ernestine Aloisia Ungnad von Weissenwolff, *1740, by Martin van Meytens the Younger. Gift of Mr. and Mrs. Nate B. Spingold, 1950. The Metropolitan Museum of Art, New York.*

RENAISSANCE DOGS

'Which one of you lucky chaps wants a wet dog in their lap?'

Discussion of Latin philosophers – Cato the Elder, Scipio, Livy and Atticus; 15th century, by artist unknown, Chateau of Chantilly, France.

In 1389, in his work *Livre de Chasse* (*Book of the Hunt*), French nobleman Gaston III de Foix detailed the life of lowly child servants called 'dog boys' who, in addition to handling all the dog-related chores, had to sleep with the dogs in the kennels all night to keep them from fighting. They were warm, at least.

4.
THE DOGHOUSE

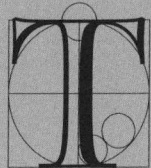HE RENAISSANCE had its fair share of both good and bad dogs. Now, for the first time in history, they were being recorded by painters who were always keen to catch them in the act. Welcome to the doghouse…

Doggy day care, 15th century, by artist unknown. © CCI/Bridgeman Images.

'Yes, I ate your cat food.'

Portrait of a Young Man With a Dog and a Cat, *c.1500, by Dosso Dossi. © Ashmolean Museum/Bridgeman Images.*

Pugs, the popular pint-sized toy dog breed, made their grand European debut during the Renaissance, brought from China by Dutch traders. A famous legend states that in 1572, a pug named Pompey saved the life of William the Silent, Prince of Orange, by alerting him to an assassination attempt. In gratitude, the pug became the official dog of the House of Orange.

THE DOGHOUSE

'Sorry, can I just squeeze through? I'm late for dinner.'

The Rise of the Calvary, *1505*, by the Master of the Pietá of Saint-Germain-des-Pres.

'The more I see of men, the better I like my dog.'

Madame Roland, 1780.

'I'll eat any scraps from the table – except penises. Yuck!'

The Reward of Cruelty, *1751, by William Hogarth.*

William Hogarth, the renowned artist, frequently featured his pug, Trump, in his paintings. A notable example is his 1745 self-portrait, *Painter and his Pug*, displayed at London's Tate Gallery. As the Tate's caption explains, Trump represented 'the artist's own pugnacious character,' highlighting Hogarth's notorious belligerence.

'I'd watch where you are walking if I was you. This is going to be a slippery one.'

A Man with Crouching Dog (Smell), 1650s, by Adriaen van Ostade.

RENAISSANCE DOGS

'Hey, wait for me. I wanna be in this one!'

Portrait of a Young Man and His Tutor, *1685, by Nicolas de Largillierre. National Gallery of Art, London.*

'Where's that stupid cat gone?'

THE DOGHOUSE

'A work of art? That's me!'

Arnolfini and his Wife, *1434, by Jan van Eyck. Bridgeman Images.*

===

Dogs were commonly depicted in Renaissance paintings to
symbolise loyalty, fidelity and protection. They would often
appear in portraits of married couples to represent faithfulness.

'Can I please swap places with someone?'

Allegory of the Elements, *1597, by Michelangelo Merisi da Caravaggio. © Raffaello Bencini/Bridgeman Images.*

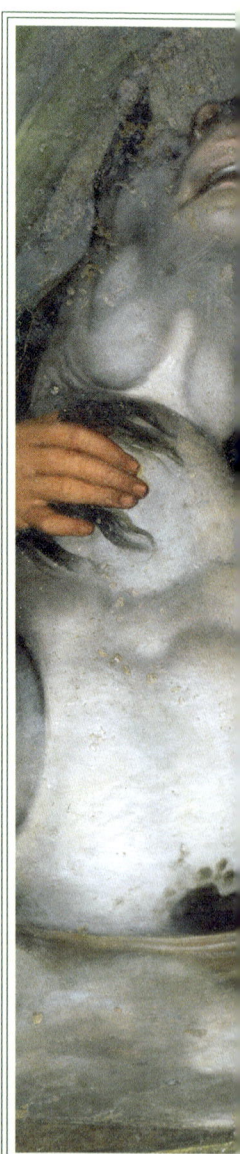

RENAISSANCE DOGS

THE DOGHOUSE

'I completely forgot what I came in here for. Don't you just hate that?'

Guardroom with the Deliverance of Saint Peter, *1645,*
by David Teniers the Younger. Bridgeman Images.

RENAISSANCE DOGS

'No wonder he's ill – I've been pooping in that bowl.'

Seven Sacraments Altarpiece, 1445–50, by Rogier van der Weyden. Wikimedia Commons.

PRO CRIMINE P.

5.
BEWARE OF THE DOG

WHEN IT COMES to protecting their family, it's not the size of the dog in the fight, but the size of the fight in the dog. From giant watchdogs to tiny, yapping alarm dogs, and every type in between, you'd better not mess with these mutts – or else!

Dog with a bone to pick, Room of Diana and Actaeon, 1524, by Francesco Mazzola (known as Parmigianino). Ghigo Roli/Bridgeman Images.

'I wouldn't get on my bad side if I were you!'

Portrait of a Gentleman, *1625, by the French School. Wikimedia Commons.*

———

Famed English diarist Samuel Pepys, writing in the late 1600s, often noted observations about dogs. On one evening, he was so entertained watching his 'little bitch' engage in amorous doggy-style with 'Mrs Buggin's little dog, the finest dog that ever I saw in my life,' that it provoked him to 'make pleasure with my wife more than usual tonight.'

'I'm bored. Can we go play outside now?'

Federigo Gonzaga, *Duke of Mantua*, 1525–30, by
Tiziano Vecellio. Bridgeman Images.

RENAISSANCE DOGS

BEWARE OF THE DOG

'You want to snuffle this belly, don't you? It's OK, I know how cute I am.'

Canina con Biscotti, *1648,*
by Giovanna Garzoni.

'If he plays "Wonderwall" one more time, I'll go barking mad!'

Musical Group on a Balcony, *1622, by Gerrit van Honthorst. Bridgeman Images.*

The Distaff Gospels, a 15th-century collection of folklore, offered peculiar pet 'life hacks'. To avoid angry dogs, give them 'good roasted cheese' while reciting the phrase '*In camo et freno, et cetera.*' ('With bit and bridle, bridle their jaws, and so on'). If a lady wanted her new suitor to get along with her family, she could secretly mix her family's dog's urine into her husband's beer; after drinking it and greeting the dog, he would become friendly with those the dog loved.

'Mess with the bull – you're gonna get the horns!'

The Adoration of the Magi, 16th century, by the Swiss School. © Fine Art Images/Bridgeman Images.

'I need a bath too, Mum. I just rolled around in my own poop.'

Bathsheba at the Bath, c.1485, by Hans Memling. © Bernard Bonnefon. All rights reserved 2025/Bridgeman Images.

John Heywood, a key 16th-century proverb collector, featured numerous Renaissance-era folk wisdom and dog-related sayings in his 1546 work, *Proverbes*. These included observations such as 'The feeblest hounds bark most' and 'No more trust than in a dog's tail'. He also noted, 'Hungry dogs will eat dirty puddings,' highlighting their love of scoffing! The phrase 'hair of the dog (that bit you)', a remedy for hangovers, also appears for the first time here.

'I guess dinner will be late tonight?'

Jesus before Herode Antipas, *panel of the altarpiece of the Master's Passion at the Carnation of Baden, c.15th century, by the Master of the Baden Carnation.*
© Photo Josse / Bridgeman Images.

BEWARE OF THE DOG

'Babies — all they do is eat, poop and whine. And that's my job!'

Nativity, 1600, by Pier Francesco Mazzucchelli.
© Mauro Ranzani/Bridgeman Images.

'Dude, what on Earth have you been eating?'

A Mastiff and a Small Dog, *1700–1799, by the British School.*

BEWARE OF THE DOG

6.
HOT DOGGIN'

DURING THE RENAISSANCE, dogs followed us everywhere, even into battle, which, when you look into the history of this period, happened *a lot*. Let us now follow them around for a bit and see what pawsome things they get up to. Remember: wherever a dog is, silliness isn't far behind.

Saint Roch, the patron saint of dogs, pointing at a dog, 1442.

'Humans are getting really good at painting now. Look at this linear perspective!'

Interior of a Hall with Figures, *1621, by Nicolaes de Gyselaer.*
© *Fitzwilliam Museum/Bridgeman Images.*

In the 1550s, King Henry III of France was so enamoured with dogs that he would sometimes employ people to steal a dog he particularly liked if its owner refused to sell it! Over his lifetime, Henry reportedly housed more than 2,000 dogs, many of them toy breeds.

HOT DOGGIN'

RENAISSANCE DOGS

HOT DOGGIN'

'Last Supper?
It better not be.'

Last Supper, 1600, by Camillo Procaccini. Mondadori Portfolio/Archivio
Magliani/Mauro Magliani & Barbara Piovan/Bridgeman Images.

HOT DOGGIN'

'Does my tongue smell of butt to you?'

A Laughing Bravo with his Dog, *1628, by Hendrick Ter Brugghen. Christie's Images/Bridgeman Images.*

RENAISSANCE DOGS

'Spot the dog!'

Portrait of a Lady holding a Dog and a Tulip, *c.1620, English School. © Richard Philp, London/Bridgeman Images.*

'This is a nice warm spot for a nap.'

'Lap me, Mum. It's where I belong.'

Our Lady of the Seven Dolours, *1490, by the Master Hoogstraeten. © Art in Flanders/Bridgeman Images.*

In 1570, John Caius, a prominent English physician, published *De Canibus Britannicis* (*Of Englishe Dogges*). In it, Caius meticulously detailed various dog types, from hunting hounds to household companions, organising dogs by their function in human society rather than just by appearance. Regarding lapdogs, he notably wrote, 'The smaller they be, the more pleasure they provoke.'

'What does the letter say? I can't see a thing!'

Husband and Wife, *c.1523, by Lorenzo Lotto, Bridgeman Images.*

In 1685, German physician and naturalist Christian Franz Paullini authored what's considered the first canine encyclopedia. Titled *Cynographia Curiosa seu Canis descriptio*, it catalogued different characteristics of dogs, including their breeds, behaviours and historical significance, blending scientific observations with curious lore from the era.

HOT DOGGIN'

'That looks yummy, yummy, yummy for my tummy, tummy, tummy.'

A Lady with a Dog, *1690, by Giuseppe Maria Crespi. Samuel H. Kress Collection.*

In around 1460, *The Names of All Manner of Hounds* recorded more than 1,000 names for dogs, including some absolutely hilarious ones, including Beste-of-all, Fyndewell, Garlik, Wellyfedde, Goodynowze, Filthe and Havegoodday.

'Something down here smells delicious.'

'If I'd known an angel from Heaven was coming, I'd have combed my hair.'

Tobias and the Angel, c.1475, by Filippino Lippi.
National Gallery of Art, London.

During the Renaissance, dogs were often used in bizarre and cruel medical remedies. To treat tuberculosis, for example, some physicians believed that boiling newborn puppies and bathing in the water absorbed the creatures' warmth.

RENAISSANCE DOGS

'This looks like it might take a while. Can I go play with my friends?'

HOT DOGGIN'

The Death of Procris, a Satyr Mourning over a Nymph, *1495, by Piero di Cosimo. Bridgeman Images.*

7.
EVERY DOG HAS ITS DAY (OFF)

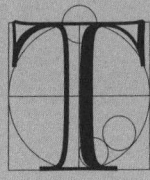HE WORLD'S GREATEST Renaissance wordsmith, William Shakespeare, once mused that 'Every dog has its day'. While that's true, it's also true that even a top dog sometimes needs a day off, too.

Diana with her (odd-looking) dog, *1670, by Ermanno Stroiffi.*
Luisa Ricciarini/Bridgeman Images.

'Catherine, I can't help but feel this was partly my fault.'

Martyrdom of Saint Catherine, 1540, by Gaudenzio Ferrari. © Pinacoteca di Brera, Milan/With permission of the Italian Ministry of Culture/Bridgeman Images.

EVERY DOG HAS ITS DAY (OFF)

'Can we hurry this along? I've got a ball that needs chasing!'

Portrait of Cornelis van Diest and his Wife, *1636, by Jacob Jordaens.*
© Derek Bayes. All rights reserved 2025/Bridgeman Images.

In June 1660, a month after his restoration, King Charles II's black spaniel-greyhound mix vanished. Outraged, the king placed an advertisement in the *Mercurius Publicus* for its return. He stated that the dog, 'not born nor bred in England' would never abandon him, adding: 'Will they never leave robbing His Majesty? Must He not keep a Dog?' The king believed the dog was stolen.

'It's a dog's life.'

Margaret Fiennes, Baroness Dacre, Wife of Sampson Lennard of Chevening, Esq, *1561, by Marcus Gheeraerts the Younger. Wikimedia Commons.*

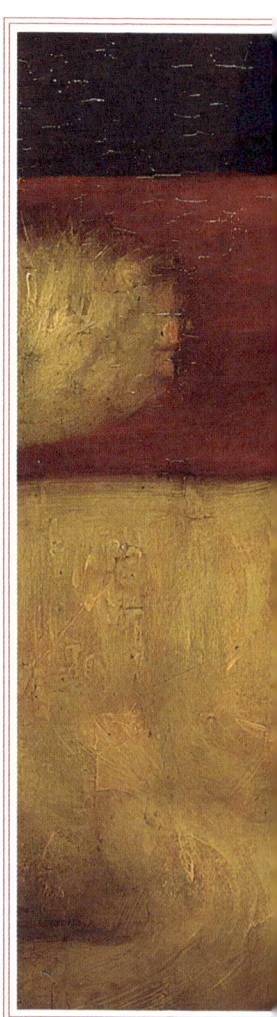

EVERY DOG HAS ITS DAY (OFF)

RENAISSANCE DOGS

'Don't judge – it's for medical purposes!'

Dog with Lilies, 1660s, by Juan de Pareja.

RENAISSANCE DOGS

EVERY DOG HAS ITS DAY (OFF)

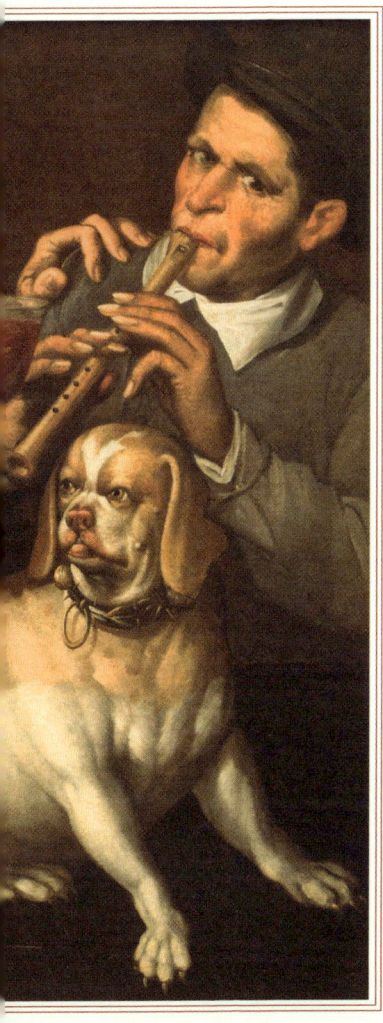

'Imagine *us* sitting on *your* lap.'

Zufolo Player, *c.1585*, by *Bartolomeo Passerotti*.

'This poor guy can't catch a break. Ooh, look, bones!'

The Entombment of Christ, *1510–1518, by Juan de Flandes.*

Mary, Queen of Scots, who ruled from six days old until 25, adored her 22 lapdogs – mainly pugs, spaniels and Maltese terriers. During her 18-year English imprisonment, her gaoler noted she spent hours each day talking to them. In a final act of devotion, a Skye terrier, hidden beneath her skirt, accompanied Mary to her 1587 execution. Found shaking and covered in blood, post-beheading, the loyal dog refused to move or eat – and died soon after.

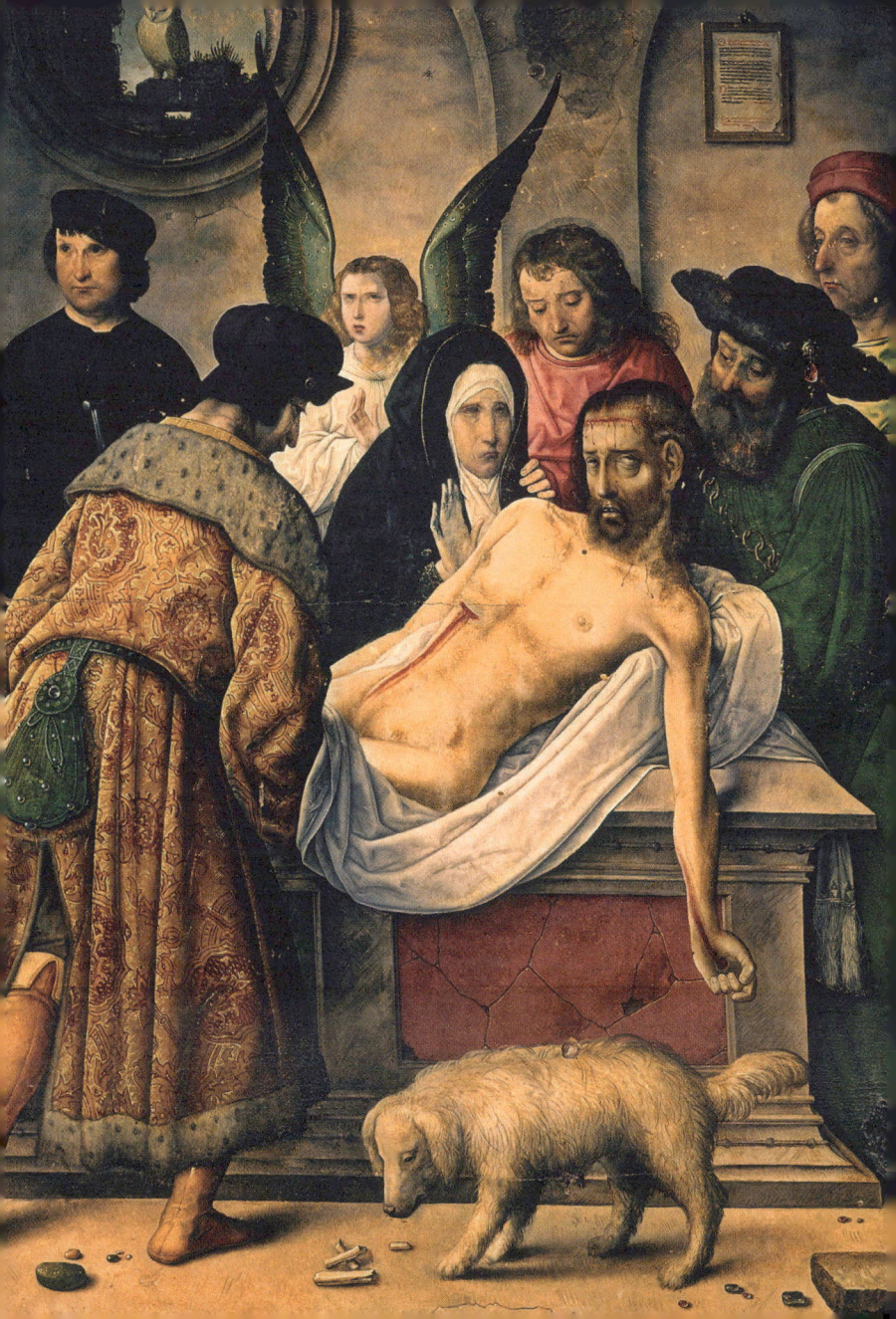

EVERY DOG HAS ITS DAY (OFF)

'Woah, guys, are you seeing these colours too? I'm tripping balls big time!'

A British trader bargains with an Indian merchant, c.1500.

'Calm down, Spanker. Mum and Dad will be home soon.'

Altarpiece of the Nativity, *16th century, by the Master of Sigmaringen.*

In 16th-century British kitchens, a small dog bred specifically to power a meat spit was a common sight. These 'turnspit dogs' ran in a hamster-like wheel, an essential fixture for roasting, for several hours. Their continuous motion ensured the meat cooked evenly over the fire.

EVERY DOG HAS ITS DAY (OFF)

'I'm cute and cuddly too... it's just on the inside.'

The Childhood and Passion of Christ, *c.1480, by Martin Schongauer.*

'Here comes the hairball.'

8.
BARKING UP THE WRONG TREE

FROM HOWLING at the moon to yapping at the postman, dogs of the Renaissance were always on high alert, ready to protect their human buddies from the dangers that lurked around every corner. They were also just absolutely barking mad…

Pluto, God of the Underworld, and his wife, Prosperine. *Detail of The Council of the Gods, 1624, by Giovanni Lanfranco © Frank Buffetrille. All rights reserved 2025/Bridgeman Images.*

RENAISSANCE DOGS

'Mum, can you put some clothes on? That man's looking at you all funny again.'

Venus with an Organist and a Dog,
c.1550, by Tiziano Vecellio.

BARKING UP THE WRONG TREE

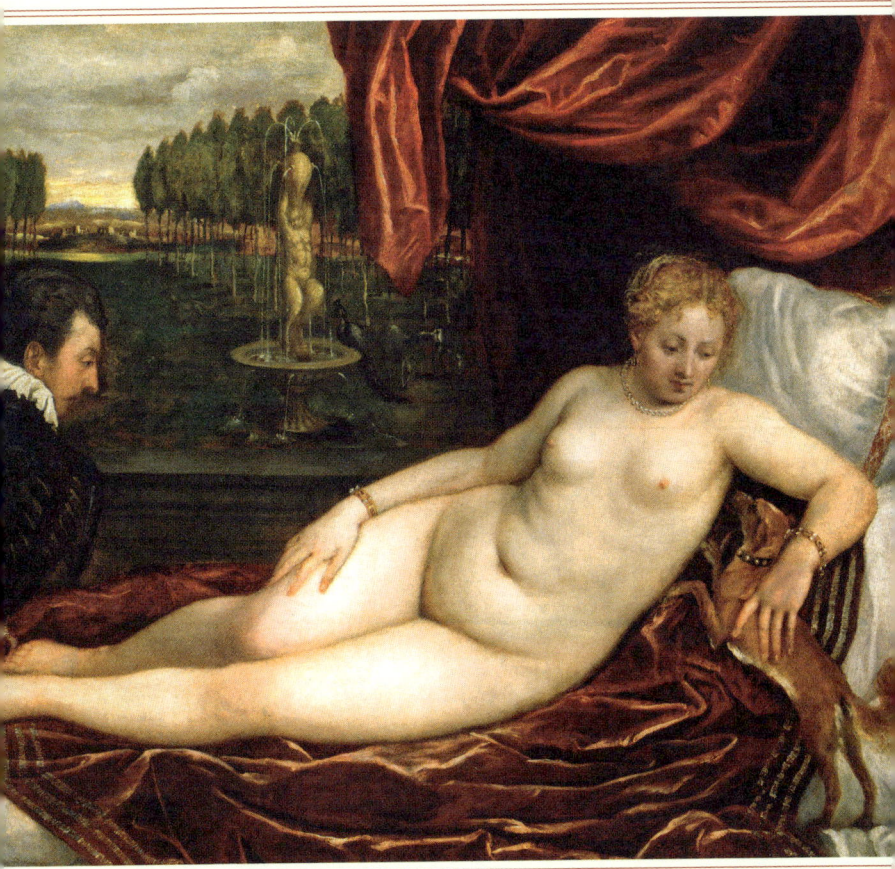

'I feel sick – call the vet quickly!'

Map of Australia, from Cosmographie Universelle, *1555, by Guillaume le Testu. Bridgeman Images.*

———

Legend claims England's last wolf was killed in 1390 by John Harrington of Wraysholme, Lancashire. While dogs are related to wolves, modern dog-scientists are now convinced both species descended from a common, extinct wolf-like ancestor. That ancestor is believed to have roamed the lands around 100,000 years ago.

RENAISSANCE DOGS

'All rise; this counsel is now in session!'

Captain Lord George Graham in his Cabin, *c.1745, by William Hogarth.*

RENAISSANCE DOGS

'I just pissed all over your dress.'

*Marie Emilie Coignet de Courson with a Dog, c.1769, by Jean Honoré Fragonard.
Fletcher Fund, 1937. The Metropolitan Museum of Art, New York.*

'I think you've had enough for tonight, Dad.'

The Jester, 1519, by Marx Reichlich. Bridgeman Images.

A dog's extraordinary nose can detect the passing of time, sense human emotions and even identify illnesses such as cancer. Its design also allows simultaneous breathing and sniffing, with each nostril working independently. This remarkable adaptation, combined with up to 50 times more scent receptors than humans, explains their unparalleled sense of smell in the animal kingdom.

RENAISSANCE DOGS

'Circumcision? That's nothing. Try being neutered.'

The Circumcision, *1500, by Marco Marziale.*

'Oi! Don't leave me out. I'm part of this family too.'

Portrait of the Gozzadini Family, *1584, by Lavinia Fontana.*

BARKING UP THE WRONG TREE

'Paint me like one of your French girls, Jack.'

A Spaniel Seated on an Embroidered Cushion, *1650, by Francesco Fieravino. © Bonhams, London/Bridgeman Images.*

RENAISSANCE DOGS

'If your name's not on the list, you're not coming in.'

Bouncer, the dog, The Sleeping Dog and the Wolf, *1480, by Gherardo del Fora. New York Digital Library Public Collections.*

ὦ οὗτος, ἴσθι ὡς ὁ ποιητὴς Λύης, φυ-
λάζομαι δ' οὐ γὰρ ἂν πέπου καρδίαν εἴληφας, ἀλλ' ἐμοὶ καρδίαν ἔδο-
κας. Ἐπιμύθιον·
ὁ μῦθος δηλοῖ, ὅτι πολλάκις τὰ
παθήματα τοῖς ἀνθρώποις μαθή-
ματα γίνου:

κύων καὶ λύκος·
ύων πρό ἐπαύλεώς τινος ἐ-
κάθευδε. λύκου δὲ ἐπιδρα-
μόντος καὶ βρῶμα μέλλοντος θέσθαι
αὐτόν, ἐδεῖτο μὴ νῦν αὐτὸν κατα-
θῦσαι. νῦν μὲν γάρ φησι λεπτός ἐ-
μι καὶ ἰσχνός. ἂν δὲ μικρὸν ἀνα-
μείνῃς, μέλλουσιν οἱ ἐμοὶ δεσπόται

9.
HOUNDS OF LOVE

DURING THE RENAISSANCE, our bond with dogs grew so strong that we elevated their relationship status from hard-working servant to ultimate best friend. We even finally decided to let them into our homes to live too, a symbol of just how essential they were to our happiness.

Portrait of a child, late 16th century, by the Italian School.
The Buccleuch Collections/Bridgeman Images, reproduced with the
kind permission of the Duke of Buccleuch & Queensberry, KT.

'And she says I'm the smelly one – the cheek of it!'

King Candaules of Lydia Showing his Wife to Gyges, 1646, by Jacob Jordaens. Wikimedia Commons.

During the Renaissance, popular dog types varied by their function. Greyhounds hunted fast game, while spaniels flushed out birds. Mastiffs guarded livestock, and scent hounds such as beagles tracked prey over long distances. Small, feisty terriers were essential for vermin control. For noblewomen, tiny status-symbol lapdogs such as Bolognese and Maltese were highly prized; indeed, the smaller the dog, the greater the perceived wealth of her husband.

'Mum, Dad, this is getting... awkward.'

Susanna and the Elders, 1561, by Alessandro Allori. Imago/
H. Tschanz-Hofmann/Bridgeman Images.

*Did you know the expression
'fight like cats and dogs' was born in the
Renaissance sometime around 1550?'*

'You put your left leg in, you take your left leg out...'

A Man Dancing with a Dog, 1655, by Hendrick Bogaert.
Rijksmuseum, Amsterdam.

'What do you mean dogs look like their owners? How rude!'

Portrait of a Lady with a Lapdog, *1570, by Girolamo Macchietti. Wikimedia Commons.*

'Quiet! Did you hear that? Someone just opened a tin.'

Jane Weston, Second Wife of Sir Thomas Bisshopp, *1610, by the English School. © Parham House/Nick McCann/Bridgeman Images.*

'I hate school! I think it's time I ate the homework.'

Circe and Her Lovers in a Landscape, *1525, by Dosso Dossi. National Gallery of Art, London.*

———

Between 1589 and 1623, dogs were mentioned more than 200 times in the masterpieces of William Shakespeare...

'Cry "Havoc!" and let slip the dogs of war.'
Mark Antony, (Act 3, Scene 1), *Julius Caesar.*

'To the right, down a bit, a bit more, under the hand, now squint really hard – there I am!'

Portrait of a Lady, 1625, The Convent of Madre de Deus.
National Museum of Ancient Art, Lisbon, Portugal.

'I don't care if it's solid gold, you're going to need a bigger pooper-scooper than *that*....'

The Theological Virtues: Faith, Charity, Hope, 1500, by an Italian (Umbrian) Painter. Purchase Bequest of Mary Cushing Fosburgh and Gift of Rodman Wanamaker, by exchange, 1982. The Metropolitan Museum of Art, New York.

'We often get confused for twins.'

Princess Varvara Nikolaevna Gagarina, *1780, by Jean-Baptiste Greuze. Gift of Mrs. William M. Haupt, from the collection of Mrs. James B. Haggin, 1965. The Metropolitan Museum of Art, New York.*

During the Renaissance, humans were busy; they invented: the printing press, flush toilet, pocket watch, musket, spinning wheel, thermoscope (early thermometer), microscope, telescope, barometer, pendulum clock, calculating machine, pencil and the diving bell.

10.
HAIR OF THE DOG

RENAISSANCE DOGS ROCKED hilarious, often wild, hairstyles, from radical half-permed poodles to shaggy-mopped mongrels and everything in between. Thanks to the era's great painters, we can now feast our eyes on these furry, fluffy coiffures in all their magnificent – and ridiculous – glory.

Aeneas at the court of Dido, *1510, by Bernardino de Donati.* © NPL – DeA Picture Library/ G. De Gregorio/Bridgeman Images.

HAIR OF THE DOG

'A pat, please. Just one. And a tummy tickle.'

Dog of the Havana Breed, *1724*,
by Jean-Jacques Bachelier.

HAIR OF THE DOG

'Dad, I think I need a haircut.'

Portrait of an Unknown Man, *1650, by artist unknown,*
Stamford and Rutland Hospital.

'Good a page as any to wipe my butt.'

RENAISSANCE DOGS

'Mum, why am I in this painting, but not that one?'

Princess Henrietta Anne Stuart, Duchess of Orléans, *1670*, by Jean Charles Nocret the younger. National Trust Photographic Library/Bridgeman Images.

DE·LVCRETIA·VALERIVS·ET·AVGVSTINVS·MIRA
LOQVNTVR·QVE·BREVITAS·OMITTI·FECIT·

Lucretia mortua omnium astantium planctus quammaximus est
leuatus. Brutus qui sapientissimum animum suum metu diu celaue
rat. accepto gladio e uulnere sic iurauit tarquinium regem et tar
quiniorum omnium nomen aburbis dominio omnino eXterminare.
Lucretius tricipitinus pater lucretiae ceteriq; mirantes nouum i
psius bruti ingenium et animum diuinum: coniurauerunt simul
illumq; ducem omnium omnino secuti sunt: ad eXtminum regis

HAIR OF THE DOG

'Admit it.
You're jealous of
this awesome hair.'

Roman History, in Latin, from the foundation of Rome to the reign of Constantine the
Great, *1450, Bibliothèque de l'Arsenal, MS-667, Bibliothèque Nationale de France.*

RENAISSANCE DOGS

'Who let the dogs out? Who, who, who?'

Dancing Dogs: 'Lusette', 'Madore', 'Rosette' and 'Moucheby', 1759, by John Wootton. © National Trust Images/Derrick E. Witty.

'I told him, "You're going to regret getting your hair cut like that." But did he listen? No.'

Santo Domingo de Guzmán, *1528, by Ambrosius Benson.*

'Would you find me cuter if I was shaved the other way round?'

Dispute of St. Catherine with the Philosophers, *1505, by artist unknown. Wikimedia Commons.*

RENAISSANCE DOGS

'Get ready to catch me, Dad – 3, 2, 1!'

Lady Archer's Maltese Terrier, *1787*, by George Stubbs.

Richard Brome, a prominent English dramatist, was perhaps the first to write the phrase 'It shall rain dogs and polecats', an early variation of the now-popular idiom 'it's raining cats and dogs', which describes heavy rainfall, in his 1652 play *The City Wit*.

'I'm happy to stay here all day if you need me to.'

Portrait of a Lady with a Dog, c.1550, by Paris Bordone.
© The Schorr Collection/Bridgeman Images.

The Virgin Mary at the Crucifixion, *c.1500*,
Bourg-Achard, Ancient Priory of St Lo, France,
by the French School. Bridgeman Images.